Little Catechism on the Eucharist

By Fr. Roberto Coggi, O.P.
with the
Institute of St. Clement I,
Pope and Martyr

Preface by J. Francis Cardinal Stafford

Foreword by Francis Cardinal George, OMI

Illustrated by
Laura Pietra
Mirko and Rosa Pellicioni

New Hope Publications

Catechism Series #1
Original Edition:
ESD (Edizioni Studio Domenicano)
in collaboration with the Institute of St. Clement I,
Pope and Martyr
www.istitutosanclemente.it
info@istitutosanctemante.it

For additional copies of this book, contact:
New Hope Publications
3050 Gap Knob Road
New Hope, KY 40052 U.S.A.
270-325-3061

ISBN #1-892875-30-6

We wish to acknowledge the graphic design assistance of Malb Studio Flaguel in Paris, France.

TABLE OF CONTENTS

PART ONE: THE GIFT OF THE EUCHARIST
(By Father Roberto Coggi, O.P.)

PART TWO: MIRACLES OF THE EUCHARIST
(By the Institute of St. Clement I, Pope and Martyr)

PART THREE: THE SAINTS AND THE EUCHARIST
(By the Institute of St. Clement I, Pope and Martyr)

Preface

The *Little Catechism on the Eucharist* is a Eucharistic compendium for young people. It is also useful for those who are seeking an initial introduction to "The Mystery of Faith," the wonderful phrase used by the Church from earliest times to describe the Sacrament of the Eucharist. It is divided into three parts.

"The Gift of the Eucharist," the first part developed by Father Roberto Coggi, O.P., places the mystery of the Eucharist within the glory of the inner-Trinitarian life and the dramatic encounter between divine freedom and human freedom at the heart of the Incarnation. Like the *Catechism of the Catholic Church,* the *Little Catechism on the Eucharist* is Trinitarian and Incarnational.

The *Little Catechism on the Eucharist* emphasizes that the Eucharist should be understood within the revelation of the Most Holy Trinity and of the Incarnation. Readers will be introduced to the most profound mystery of all reality: the inner Trinitarian life. They will learn that God's Being is a life of loving and eternal self-giving. They will be called to confess that God, by His nature and essence, is the surrender of Himself within the eternal processions of the three divine Persons: the absolute self-giving of the Father to the otherness of the Son, of the Son to the Father and of both to the Holy Spirit. The *Little Catechism on the Eucharist* teaches that the Incarnation of the Son mirrors that inner life. Jesus glorifies the Father by allowing Himself to be the One through whom the Father's love is revealed to the world, and the Father and the Holy Spirit glorify the Son by raising Him from the dead.

Readers will further discover that the Incarnation was for the sake of Jesus's "hour" which encompassed both His crucifixion and the Last Supper. God the Father handed over His incarnate Son for our sake. St. Gregory of Nyssa has offered the Church the extraordinary fruit of his meditations on this mystery: "Because of death, God took upon Himself to be born."

The Eucharist is the greatest sacrament of God's self-giving. Jesus gave Himself, fully and without reserve, when He said over the bread and the cup of wine, "This is my Body given up for you, this is my Blood poured out for you." And this loving and incredible form of the Son's self-giving in total freedom to the Father for the sake of sinners is repeated sacramentally whenever a priest celebrates the Eucharist. In suggesting the substance of the readers' response to this Good News, the *Little Catechism on the Eucharist* takes its clue from St. Paul: "Do nothing from selfishness or conceit, but in humility count others better than yourselves. Let each of you look not only to his own interests, but also to the interests of others." Being Christ's Body, baptized readers are called to participate in the total self-giving of the Eucharistic Lord. Those who know themselves to be seriously falling short of that self-surrender to God's will by mortal sin are instructed by the *Little Catechism on the Eucharist* about the necessity of recourse to the Sacrament of Confession.

The first part of the *Little Catechism on the Eucharist* is thus a catechetical unfolding of the sublime truth of "the bread of angels, bread from heaven, the medicine of immortality." Together with the *Little Catechism on the Eucharist*, the sixth chapter of the Gospel of John, cited in the text, requires many hours of meditation and prayer. That sixth chapter is a high-point in the revelation of the Eucharist.

Its second and third parts—"Eucharistic Miracles" and "Eucharistic Saints"—were developed by the Institute of St. Clement I, Pope and Martyr. Various Eucharistic

miracles are cited from the tradition. I was especially edi-
fied upon rereading, after many decades, the Eucharistic
experiences of the saints. I still vividly recall the impact
upon myself of the story of St. Tarcisius, "the boy martyr
of the Eucharist" killed in the third century. The third part
of the *Little Catechism on the Eucharist* cites him as a
model. I first heard of St. Tarcisius's Eucharistic faith and
courage in 1939, the year of the outbreak of the Second
World War. We were preparing to receive our first Holy
Communion in May 1940. Sr. Mary Irene, SSND, told her
fascinated second graders about the Eucharistic circum-
stances of his martyrdom. St. Tarcisius has been a model
for me ever since. Later, I learned that the facts of his
violent death have been handed down by Pope St. Damasus
I. By God's providence, my work at the Apostolic Penitentiary in Rome is located on the site of that Pope's boyhood
home which he later converted into the papal chancellory
in about 380 AD.

These final two parts of the *Little Catechism on the
Eucharist,* even though not formally doctrinal, are supple-
mentary and significant aids in Eucharistic catechesis.

J. Francis Cardinal Stafford
Major Penitentiary
Vatican City
February 10, 2005
Memorial of St. Scholastica, Virgin

Foreword

This *Little Catechism on the Eucharist* is a worthwhile project. It is also ambitious. As well as setting out the teaching of the Church on the Eucharist, it puts it in the context of the Christian faith, beginning with the existence of God, the mystery of the Trinity, the Incarnation of Jesus Christ and the Church with her teaching role. It is a practical reminder that the Eucharist is to be understood in the light of revelation. "That in this sacrament are the true Body of Christ and the true Blood is something that 'cannot be apprehended by the senses,'" says St. Thomas Aquinas, "but only by faith which relies on divine authority" (CCC 1381).

This Catechism ensures that a student's faith in the Eucharist is informed and is sound. As one would expect from a Dominican author, the theological explanation given of key ideas such as sacrifice, sacrament, presence, and transubstantiation is faithful to the teaching of St. Thomas Aquinas. It is clear, yet respects the depths of the mystery.

This book is a gift to parents, teachers and catechists at a time of religious ignorance and confusion. It could be useful to homilists. It inculcates a practical devotion to the Eucharist of a kind that supports Catholic teaching and is calculated to enable us to "experience in ourselves the fruitfulness of redemption." (Prayer for Corpus Christi)

Eucharistic devotion is illustrated by accounts of miracles which give evidence of popular piety at various periods of history and which are always to be read in the context of the Church's doctrine.

The section on the Saints and the Eucharist shows how closely exceptional holiness is often linked to devotion to the Blessed Sacrament.

Those teaching from this Catechism should also make good use of the *Catechism of the Catholic Church* (1322-1419), the encyclical of Pope John Paul II, *Ecclesia de Eucharistia,* and his Apostolic Letter for the Year of the Eucharist, *Mane Nobiscum Domine.*

May all who use this Catechism find their faith strengthened and their love for the Blessed Sacrament of the altar deepened.

Francis Cardinal George, OMI
Archbishop of Chicago

Praise from Other Cardinals and Bishops...

The Holy Eucharist is at the center of the Church's life (cf. *Ecclesia de Eucharistia,* 3). The Eucharistic Sacrifice is fount and apex of the whole Christian life (cf. *Lumen Gentium,* 11). It is therefore very important that introduction into the faith and practice of the Church regarding the Holy Eucharist be given great prominence in catechesis.

The *Little Catechism on the Eucharist* is very welcome and is highly commendable, because it presents the Eucharistic Sacrifice and Sacrament to the young in a sound, attractive and pedagogically wise format.

Basic truths of our faith regarding the Holy Eucharist are stated with clarity. Accounts of some miracles regarding this august mystery, although not demanding faith assent as accounts, can help our faith. And examples of Saints specially devoted to the Holy Eucharist are uplifting.

I congratulate the Edizioni Studio Domenicano and the Istituto San Clemente I Papa e Martire for this work and its distribution.

This booklet arrives as the Holy Father declared today a Eucharistic Year. May it bring many graces to children and to some adults too.

Francis Cardinal Arinze
Prefect of the Congregation for the Divine
Worship and the Discipline of the Sacraments

...The little volume has this added benefit: color paintings which enrich the text will be of great help to children, imprinting the fundamental concepts of their faith on children's minds.

Here we have a book which is most useful and up-to-date. What the Edizioni Studio Domenicano set out to do is, in fact, to help overcome the ignorance and superficiality which is often to be seen in our way of speaking of the Sacrifice of the Altar and our participation in it. Not infrequently, faith in the Real Presence and in transubstantiation is more or less lost in the shadows, with all the consequent effects which are deadly to an authentic Christian life.

My hope is that this work will accomplish its goal, that is, reviving in its readers that faith and devotion towards that *"Sacramentum amoris"* which the Lord, before ascending to the Father, wanted to leave us as his most precious testament.

José Cardinal Saraiva Martins
Prefect of the Congregation for the Causes of the Saints

...I rejoice at this important initiative to propose the principal mysteries of our faith in an adequate manner. For this reason I hope it will be widely distributed and will thus contribute, as it is written, to "reviving in all greater faith and devotion towards the Mystery of the Eucharist."

Archbishop Stanislaus Dziwisz
(Personal Secretary to John Paul II)

The *Little Catechism on the Eucharist* is an invaluable resource for our young people. Its inviting style and careful attention to the Church's teaching provide a solid catechesis on the Eucharist in three parts: the Gift of the Eucharist, Miracles of the Eucharist, and the Saints and the Eucharist. Each part offers a clear and engaging explanation of an aspect of Eucharistic theology in prose suitable to a youthful readership. I highly recommend the *Little Catechism on the Eucharist* to all our young Catholics.

Edward Cardinal Egan (New York, NY)

Congratulations on publishing your most appropriate book setting forth what the Church teaches about Eucharist and Real Presence. May the Eucharistic Lord bless and multiply the effectiveness of this valuable publication many times over.

William H. Cardinal Keeler (Baltimore, MD)

The Most Holy Eucharist is the source, summit, and center of the lives of Catholics. This is true not only during a year proclaimed for the Eucharist, but for every year, day and moment of our lives. This book, the *Little Catechism on the Eucharist,* is an excellent teaching instrument and resource. Its enjoyable and easy style makes it a treasured gift for anyone seeking to better understand and appreciate the Church's teaching and tradition related to the Real Presence of Our Lord and Savior, Jesus Christ, in the Eucharist.

Archbishop John J. Myers (Newark, NJ)

The Eucharist is "the source and summit" of our Catholic faith. The *Little Catechism on the Eucharist* will lead both children and adults to a deeper faith in the real presence of Jesus Christ in the Eucharist. The inclusion of the witness of Eucharistic miracles throughout the ages is a help for all the faithful to recognize the constant teaching of the Church handed on from generation to generation that Jesus Christ is truly and substantially present in the Eucharist. I recommend this small compendium to all Catholics, most especially those preparing their children for first Holy Communion.

Bishop Samuel J. Aquila (Fargo, ND)

PART ONE

THE GIFT
OF THE EUCHARIST

(By Father Roberto Coggi, O.P.)

"Let the children come to me...for to such belongs the kingdom of heaven" (Mt 19:14).

The Truths of Faith

1. *Why must we believe in the Eucharist?*

Because the Eucharist is a truth of faith.

2. *What does "truth of faith" mean?*

It means a truth which God has communicated to us, speaking to us as friends to whom He wanted to reveal His secrets.

3. *How do we know that the truths of faith are real truths?*

We know this because God, who revealed them to us, can neither deceive nor be deceived. He cannot be deceived because He is infinitely intelligent and wise, and He cannot deceive us because He is infinitely good and thus cannot will to harm us.

Jesus and the Apostles

4. To whom did Jesus reveal these truths?

Jesus revealed these truths first of all to the Apostles, giving them the task of teaching them to the whole world until the end of time.

5. How could the twelve Apostles, who were mortal men, continue to teach these truths to the end of time?

They could not do it personally, but they appointed successors for this purpose, that is, men who, at their death, took their place and carried out their mission.

6. Who are the successors of the Apostles?

The Bishops headed by the Pope.

The Successors of the Apostles: The Bishops with the Pope at their head

The Holy Spirit

7. How do we know that the Bishops united with their head, the Pope, are never mistaken when teaching us the truths that God has revealed?

We are sure that they are never mistaken because Jesus promised them the help of the Holy Spirit. For this reason we can and must say that the teaching of the Bishops united with their head, the Pope, is infallible. Jesus said, "He who hears you hears me; and he who rejects you, rejects me" (Lk 10:16).

8. What do we call the truths infallibly taught by the Pope and the Bishops?

We call them dogmas of faith.

9. How many dogmas of faith are there?

They are rather numerous, and they have been formulated in the course of the centuries mainly as answers to errors that arose among Christians.

10. Are the dogmas that the Church requires us to believe restrictions on our freedom?

On the contrary, dogmas are a great help to us. Just as road signs save us from going over the cliff, so the dogmas of faith prevent us from falling into error.

We must always thank God for the dogmas He has revealed to us, and we must be grateful to the Church for expressing them in such a clear and precise way.

Just like road signs, dogmas of faith
prevent us from going over the cliff

11. **Why does the Church formulate dogmas when we already have the Scriptures, that is, the Bible, especially the Gospels?**

The Church formulates dogmas because the Scriptures must be explained. In fact, history proves that many people have interpreted the Scriptures in their own way and in ways contradictory to each other. If the Church were not there to tell us which is the correct explanation, we would always be in doubt.

12. If a person rejects a dogma of faith, can he still consider himself a Catholic Christian?

No. To be a Catholic Christian one must firmly believe all the dogmas of faith without exception. If a person rejects even one dogma of faith, that means he does not accept the God's authority or the Church's authority, and that means he no longer has faith. If I doubt even one thing revealed to me by a friend who gives me his word that it is true, that means I don't believe him and that I therefore doubt all the other things he may have told me. Thus I would no longer have faith in him. So a person who doubts even one dogma no longer has faith in God.

The Scriptures are divided into the Old Testament and the New Testament and are composed of 73 books.

Jesus is the fulfillment of the Old and New Testaments.

The Pope and the College of Bishops, with the help of the Holy Spirit,
guide the Church

The Unity and Trinity of God

The Death of Jesus

The Incarnation

The Resurrection of Jesus

The Passion of Our Lord Jesus Christ

The Principal Truths

13. **What are the principal truths of our faith?**

The Unity and Trinity of God, and the Incarnation, Passion, Death and Resurrection of Our Lord Jesus Christ.

14. **Can we only know these truths through faith?**

The existence of only one God can be discovered by reason alone without the help of faith, but only through faith do we know that there is only one God in three Persons and that the second Person became incarnate; we know this only because God has revealed it to us.

15. **How can reason discover the existence of God?**

Reason can discover this by starting from the existence of things. Things are changeable; they begin and they come to an end. Therefore their existence has no explanation unless there is a supreme, unchangeable Being. Furthermore, if we think of the extraordinary complexity and admirable order especially of all living beings, we must necessarily admit that these beings have been planned by a Supreme Mind. The order of the universe tells us of the existence of an Organizer. Because this order is within the things themselves, this Organizer must also be the Creator of these things.

The marvels of creation show us God's greatness.

We can also prove the existence of God this way: in this world good people often suffer while bad people have an easy life. This is unfair and unjust in our eyes. So there must be a Supreme Judge who will reward the good and punish evil in the next life. The Supreme Judge is God. If God is denied, the whole moral order collapses. "If God does not exist, anything goes," a great Russian novelist wrote.

16. **What can we say of the Blessed Trinity?**

The Blessed Trinity is a dogma revealed by God. Our reason alone could never discover it. It is the first principal truth of our faith.

Only God can create things out of nothing! Mother can make an omelet, but she needs eggs laid by the hen which God created.

The Blessed Trinity: Father, Son and Holy Spirit

17. Wherein does the mystery lie?

The mystery lies in the truth that only one God exists in three Persons equal yet distinct—the Father, the Son and the Holy Spirit.

18. How is it possible for three distinct beings to be only one thing?

This concept becomes clearer through the following example: think of an equilateral triangle. The three angles are the same surface (the angle is part of a plane, that is, of a surface, as we say in geometry). They are the same surface, yet the angles are distinct from one another and cannot be confused with one another. It is the same with the three divine Persons, Father, Son and Holy Spirit; they are only one God, yet they are distinct from one another and cannot be confused with one another.

In the equilateral triangle the three angles are the same surface, yet distinct from one another and cannot be confused with one another.

So are the three divine Persons, the Father, the Son and the Holy Spirit; they are only one God, yet they are distinct from one another and cannot be confused with one another.

19. **What is the second principal truth of our faith?**

The second principal truth of our faith is the Incarnation, Passion, Death and Resurrection of Our Lord Jesus Christ.

20. **What does "Incarnation" mean?**

"Incarnation" means that the second divine Person, that is, the Son, begotten of the Father before all ages, that is to say eternally, at one point took on human nature and, without ceasing to be God, became man as well.

This is what we say in the Creed: "The Son, eternally begotten of the Father..., was born of the Virgin Mary, and became man," of course without ceasing to be God. Therefore Jesus Christ is only one Person, the Son or the Word, having two natures: a divine nature which belongs to Him from all eternity, and a human nature which belongs to Him from the moment of His Incarnation.

21. **Where does this truth of our faith appear in the Gospel?**

It appears every time that Jesus, who was true man, that is, having a true human nature, declares that He is also God. For example, He says: "The Father and I are one" (Jn 10:30). Another example is His approval of St. Thomas the Apostle's profession of faith: "My Lord and my God!" (Jn 21:28)

22. **Are there many dogmas of faith regarding the Eucharist?**

Jesus is Lord of Heaven and Earth

Yes, the Church teaches many things about the Eucharist; one dogma alone would not be sufficient to express this mystery.

23. If someone wants to deepen his knowledge of the mystery of the Eucharist, where should he start?

He should start with the Gospels, letting himself be guided in his reading by the Church's teachings. He will come to see that all the Eucharistic dogmas are simply the clear and true explanation of what the Gospel says.

Before the time of Jesus, who left His teaching for us in the Gospel, the Jewish people fed on manna, which was a clear foreshadowing of the gift of the Eucharist.

The Hebrew people were freed from slavery to the Egyptians, and in the new Passover, recalled in every Eucharist, Jesus comes to bring all to salvation.

In the Old Testament, Melchisedek, priest of the Most High God, offered Him bread and wine, figures of the Eucharist (cf. Gn 14:18-20).

The blood of the lamb sprinkled on the doorposts prefigured the Blood of Jesus shed for us, which is made present in every Eucharist (cf. Es 12:1-14).

The sacrifice of Isaac prefigured the Sacrifice of the Cross made present in every Eucharist (cf. Gn 22:1-18).

The Promise of the Eucharist

24. **When is the Eucharist first mentioned in the Gospel?**

The promise of the Eucharist is first mentioned in Chapter 6 of St. John's Gospel. It is interesting to note that this promise comes right after two miracles, reported in the same chapter, which show Jesus' power over nature. The two miracles are the multiplication of the loaves and the miracle of His walking on the water across the Sea of Tiberias.

In this way Jesus prepared His disciples to accept the great Eucharistic mystery. He who had the power to multiply loaves and to walk on water would also have the power to change bread and wine into His Body and Blood.

25. **How did Jesus promise the Eucharist?**

He promised it by saying, among other things: "The bread that I will give is my flesh for the life of the world.... He who eats my flesh and drinks my blood has life everlasting, for my flesh is food indeed and my blood is drink indeed" (cf. Jn 6:51-57).

26. Can we interpret these words in a symbolic way, or just as a manner of speaking?

No. When the people objected: "This is a hard saying. Who can listen to it?", Jesus did not say: "You misunderstood me; I was only speaking symbolically." Instead He confirmed His words in such a way that many people left scandalized. Jesus did not back down, but said to His Apostles: "Do you also wish to go away?" Thus He showed them that He would rather let them go than change what He had said (cf. Jn 6:59-68).

27. What are we to conclude from this?

We must conclude that Jesus had proclaimed a great mystery; that is, He would give us His flesh to eat and His blood to drink. However, Jesus did not say how that would happen (under the appearances of bread and wine) but left this in the shadows of mystery. So we must admire the great faith of St. Peter and the other Apostles, because, even though they did not understand Jesus' words, they trusted Him blindly. Only during the Last Supper did they become aware that Jesus would offer them His Body and Blood under the appearances of bread and wine.

The Crossing of the Sea of Tiberias   The Multiplication of the Loaves

The Last Supper and the Real Presence

28. What happened during the Last Supper?

An extraordinary event took place. Jesus took the bread, blessed it, broke it and gave it to the Apostles, saying: "Take and eat; this is my Body." Then He took the cup of wine and gave it to the Apostles, saying: "All of you drink of this: for this is my Blood" (Mt 26:26).

29. Here again, could we not interpret these words in a symbolic manner, namely, that bread and wine symbolically represent the Body and Blood of Jesus?

No. First of all, Jesus clearly refers to the promise of the Eucharist, when He had expressed Himself in a realistic manner, not in a symbolic way. Furthermore, we must remember that the Apostles, being simple, rough fishermen, always took Jesus' words literally. Jesus knew this, and if He had wanted His words to be taken symbolically, He certainly would have said so. Instead, Jesus spoke those words without any explanation, which clearly means that He wanted His words to be understood just as He had spoken them.

The Last Supper

30. **What exactly do Jesus' words mean?**

Jesus' words should be understood in this way: the reality which I hold in my hands was bread before and is now my Body; in the same way, the cup which I hold in my hands previously contained wine, but now contains my Blood.

31. **So the bread and wine are no longer there?**

Exactly: the bread and wine no longer exist because the Body and Blood of Jesus have taken their place.

32. Why do I still see bread and wine? And why don't they taste different when I receive Communion?

You still see the *appearances* or the *species* of bread and wine. That is, you see the color of bread and wine and you taste bread and wine, and so on for all the senses. Yet the reality which underlies the appearances has radically changed: it was bread and wine before, and now it is the Body and Blood of Jesus.

33. Is it possible for bread and wine to exist together with the Body and Blood of Jesus?

This is impossible, as we can see by looking at Jesus' words. Jesus did not say: "This is my Body together with bread," but He said: "This," namely, this reality which I hold in my hands, "is my Body." That means, it is nothing more than my Body. Hence the bread no longer exists.

34. What happened to it?

It became the Body of Jesus. In the same way, the wine became the Blood of Jesus.

35. Did a change occur?

Yes, a very special change occurred, one with a very special name: *Transubstantiation*.

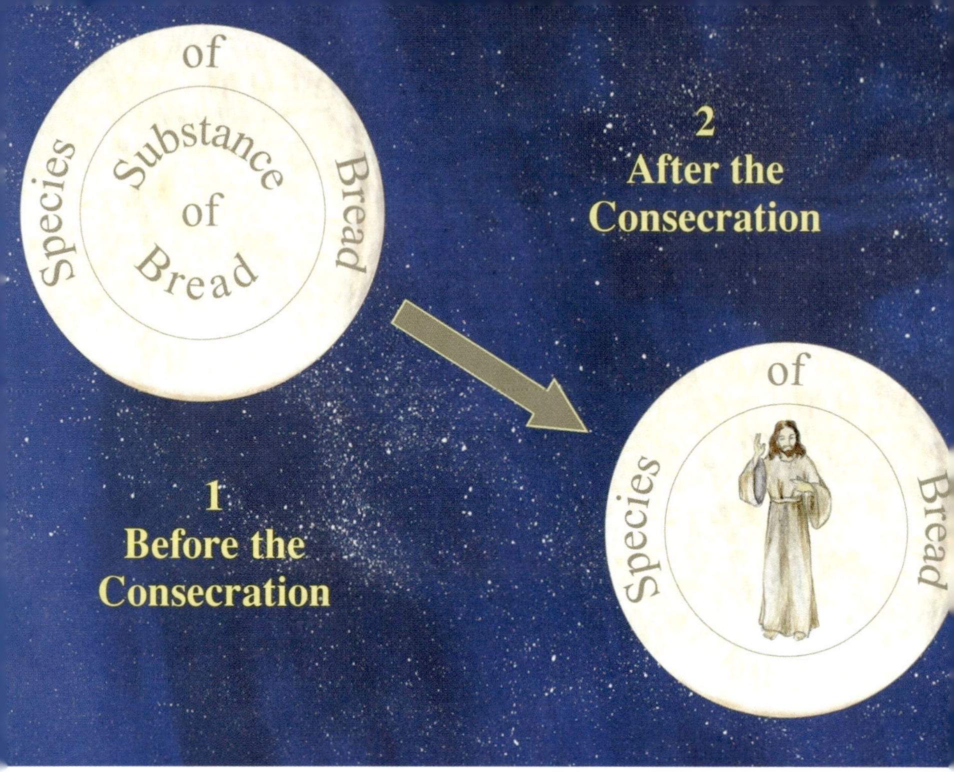

of

Substance of Bread

Species

Bread

2
After the
Consecration

of

Species

Bread

1
Before the
Consecration

Transubstantiation: before the Consecration and after the Consecration
By breaking the Host we do not break the Body of Jesus,
which is whole and entire in every single piece.

Transubstantiation

36. What does the word "transubstantiation" mean?

It means passing *(trans)* of substance *(substantia).*

37. What is substance?

Substance is a reality existing in itself and not in something else. For instance, a tree, a cat, a man are substances because they exist in themselves. On the other hand, their dimensions, colors and characteristics are certainly realities, yet these do not exist in themselves but in something else. For instance, the cat's color does not exist in itself but in the cat. We say, then, that color is not a substance but something that exists in substance and belongs to substance. Philosophers call these things *accidents;* the word comes from the Latin *accidere,* which means *to occur, to happen.* The accidents, so to speak, happen to substance. Yet, since *accidents* is a difficult word, we commonly say *species,* that is, appearances.

The ball in the picture changes color while its substance remains unchanged. In the Eucharist, on the other hand, the color and all the appearances remain unchanged, while the substance changes.

38. **What does this mean when we apply it to the Eucharist?**

It means that in the Eucharist the substance of bread and wine becomes the Body and Blood of Jesus, while the species or appearances of bread and wine remain unchanged. Hence the dimensions, color, smell and taste of the Host do not change because they are accidents or species, whereas the substance changes. We can say the same thing of the wine.

39. **When does this change occur?**

It occurs when the priest pronounces the words of consecration. When the priest has finished saying: "This is my Body," the bread no longer exists, and in its place there is the Body of Jesus. When the priest has finished saying: "This is my Blood," the wine no longer exists, and in its place there is the Blood of Jesus.

40. How is it possible for this change to occur?

It is possible by God's almighty power. When the priest pronounces the words of consecration, God intervenes with all His power and brings about the change, that is, the transubstantiation.

If we really think about it, we would not find this too surprising. If God can create everything out of nothing, why can't He change one thing into another?

41. How can the species, or the appearances of bread and wine, still exist when their substance no longer exists?

They exist miraculously, maintained by the power of God.

42. Does Jesus leave Heaven to come to us under the species of bread and wine?

No, Jesus does not leave Heaven, yet He truly comes down to us under the species of bread and wine.

43. How is this possible?

It is transubstantiation itself that makes this extraordinary fact possible. Bread and wine become the same Body and Blood which are in Heaven; they become Jesus Himself, living and real, who is seated at the right hand of His Father. Hence Jesus neither changes nor leaves Heaven, but the bread and wine, by the power of the words of consecration, become the same Jesus who is in Heaven.

44. So the same Jesus is present in the Tabernacle as in Heaven?

Yes, Jesus is in the Blessed Sacrament just as He is in Heaven, with this difference, however: in the Blessed Sacrament He is present under the species of bread and wine and is therefore invisible to us.

45. Isn't it amazing to think that the Jesus who is in the Tabernacle is the same Jesus who is at the right hand of His Father?

Yes, it is amazing, and it shows how much Jesus loves us, since He wishes to remain really and physically present among us so that we can visit Him anytime. Yet, we too often forget this marvelous gift and we do not go to visit Jesus in the Blessed Sacrament often.

46. How long is Jesus present under the Eucharistic species?

Jesus is present as long as these species maintain the appearances of bread and wine. Therefore, when we receive the Sacred Host, Jesus remains present within us until the Eucharistic species are completely absorbed and digested by our body. Normally the Eucharistic species last for about a quarter of an hour after Communion. We should remember this and stay a little while in conversation with Jesus, instead of leaving the church right after Communion.

The story is told that St. Philip Neri once ordered two altar boys, still holding candles, to go after someone who had left the church right after Communion.

47. Is Jesus present even in a tiny piece of the Host?

Yes, Jesus is there as long as that tiny piece maintains the appearances of bread. By the way, if we choose to receive Communion by receiving the Host in the hand (if we wish we can also receive It directly on the tongue), we must be careful that not even a tiny piece is left in the hand. If this happens, we must put the piece in our mouth, too. We should be most respectful of the Holy Eucharist!

48. When we break the Host, do we break the Body of Jesus as well?

No, only the Eucharistic species breaks.

29

49. How is that possible?

It is possible because Jesus is in every single piece of the consecrated Host. So, even if a part of the Host is broken, it still contains the whole Jesus.

50. According to the words of consecration, only Jesus' Body should be present under the species of bread and only His Blood should be present under the species of wine. Is this the case?

We must be careful in our choice of words. It is true that the words of consecration make the Body of Jesus directly present under the species of bread and His Blood under the species of wine, but we must not forget that the Body and Blood are inseparably united in Jesus, who is alive in Heaven. Now, the real and living Jesus is present in the Eucharist; therefore, under the species of bread, together with His Body, there must necessarily be His Blood, and where the Blood is, the Body must also necessarily be.

This is a so-called *indirect presence*, which we call a *concomitant* presence, in the sense that one presence "accompanies" the other. The presence of the Blood accompanies the presence of the Body, while the presence of the Body accompanies the presence of the Blood. And *concomitantly*, where the Body and the Blood are present, there the soul and divinity are also present. Therefore we must say that (whether under the species of bread or under the species of wine) the whole Jesus, that is, His Body, Blood, Soul and Divinity, is present.

The Mass

51. **What is the Mass?**

The Mass is the Eucharist as sacrifice.

Before the Consecration

After the Consecration

52. **What is a sacrifice?**

A sacrifice is the offering of a victim to God by a priest in our name, as a sign of our submission to Him and as an act of thanksgiving, of atonement for our sins and as a petition for graces. We say that the death of Jesus on the cross is a sacrifice because He offered Himself up to God as a victim in expiation of our sins. For this reason, in the sacrifice of the cross Jesus is at one and the same time the priest (the one who offers the sacri-

The (bloody) sacrifice of the cross is the same (unbloody) sacrifice that comes about during Holy Mass

fice) and the victim (namely the one who is being offered). The sacrifice of the cross is the central and fundamental sacrifice of the whole Christian religion. It replaces and abolishes all the sacrifices offered in the Old Testament before the coming of Christ.

53. Why do we have the Sacrifice of the Mass when we already have the sacrifice of the cross?

The Mass makes the sacrifice of Jesus on the cross present to us. The sacrifice that occurred on Calvary, outside Jerusalem, twenty centuries ago, is mysteriously made present again here and now every time Mass is celebrated.

That is why we say that the Mass is a memorial of the sacrifice of the cross. It is a remembrance, but at the same time more than that: during the sacrifice of the Mass, Jesus offers Himself to God again, renewing the offering He made on the cross. Thus when we participate in the Mass, we receive the fruit of Jesus' Passion.

54. Is the Mass important?

The Mass is the most important thing in our Christian life. There is nothing more important than Jesus' death on the cross, which merited eternal salvation for us and opened the gates of Heaven. Therefore the Mass, which applies the fruits of Jesus' death on the cross to us, is the most important and most beautiful thing in this world.

55. But isn't the Resurrection of Christ important, too?

Of course, but Jesus rose because He died first. The expiation of our sins took place on the cross.

56. Does the Resurrection have anything to do with the Mass?

Yes, because if Jesus had not risen, then there would be no Mass.

57. Why would there be no Mass?

Jesus rises from the tomb

"Bring here your finger, and see my hands; and put out your hand, and place it in my side, and be not unbelieving, but believe." Thomas answered him, "My Lord and my God!" (Jn 20:27-28)

Think of the words of consecration: the priest does not say, "This is the Body of Jesus"; he says, "This is my Body." He does not say, "This is the Blood of Jesus"; he says, "This is my Blood." This means that Jesus is the one who really says these words. Jesus consecrates the bread and wine through the priest; in other words, the priest lends Jesus his mouth and hands. On numerous occasions various saints, at the moment of consecration, saw Jesus in the place of the priest at Mass. We cannot see Jesus, but we know this is true because our faith tells us so.

The true celebrant of the Mass is the risen and living Jesus

58. What does the Resurrection of Jesus have to do with what we were discussing before?

If Jesus had not risen, He could not celebrate the Mass. But we saw that it is really He. This is proclaimed in the words of the faithful after the consecration: "We proclaim your death, Lord Jesus" (as we previously said, the Mass is the memorial of Jesus' death on the cross); "we proclaim your resurrection" (because the risen Jesus is the one celebrating Mass); "we await your coming" (because Jesus will continue to be present during the celebration of Mass till the end of the world). The Resurrection is also related to the Mass for the simple reason that if the Body and Blood of the risen Jesus were not around today, the bread and wine could not become the Body and Blood of Jesus. How could they become something that didn't exist any more?

59. If Jesus is the true celebrant of the Mass, is the celebrating priest still important?

In one sense, no, because it makes no difference whether the priest is holy or not (because Jesus will still be the main celebrant), but in another sense he is very important because there must be a priest to celebrate Mass. In fact, Jesus entrusted and gave the power to consecrate, that is, to celebrate Mass, only to priests who have received Holy Orders.

60. So is it important for us to have priests?

It is not only important—it is indispensable. If there were no priests, the Eucharist would no longer exist. This is why we must pray for vocations to the priest-

hood and, if we are young men, be open to following Jesus' call, if we hear it in our hearts, so that no place on earth will have too few priests, or even worse, no priests at all. That would be the worst thing that could happen to Christians, because the Eucharist and confession, which makes us worthy of participating in the Eucharist, would no longer be available.

Just as He did with the disciples of Emmaus, Jesus reveals Himself to us in the breaking of the bread in every Eucharist: "Their eyes were opened and they knew Him" (Lk 24:31).

61. When the priest celebrates Mass, are we just spectators?

No, we are also participants. It is true that only the priest can consecrate, as we already saw. Nonetheless the faithful, participating in the Mass, join him in offering the sacrifice; that is, they join him in offering the Body and Blood of Jesus to the Father. In fact, if we pay attention, we will notice that the priest speaks in the plural: "*We* offer you his Body and Blood"; "*We* thank you for counting us worthy to stand in your presence and serve you," and so on. The priestly service we are talking about is not consecrating bread and wine, which is reserved only to priests who have received Holy Orders, but is the offering of the already consecrated Body and Blood of Jesus.

62. Does the priestly service of the faithful consist only in the offering of the Body and Blood of Jesus to the Father?

No; we are all invited to offer ourselves together with the Body and Blood of Jesus. We must be not only priests but also victims, joined together with Jesus, the Divine Victim.

The Parts of the Mass

The Consecration

Epiclesis: Invocation
of the Holy Spirit

Before the consecration
of the bread

After the consecration
of the bread

Before the consecration
of the wine

After the consecration of the wine

The Eucharist as Sacrament

63. Is the Eucharist only real presence and sacrifice?

No, the Eucharist is also a sacrament.

64. What is a sacrament?

A sacrament is an outward sign, instituted by Jesus Christ, which confers grace on the soul.

Jesus loves us with an infinite love, but we often refuse His help

65. What is grace?

Grace is a marvelous gift of God which makes our souls bright and radiant with God's own light. Like the red-hot iron which, while remaining iron, takes on certain properties of fire, so a soul in grace, though remaining a soul, that is, a created reality, acquires certain divine qualities.

St. Catherine of Siena said that if we could see a soul in the state of grace we would think it was God Himself.

66. Does the state of grace concern only our present life, or does it concern our future life as well?

Grace is given to us in this life, but when the soul leaves this world at the moment of death, grace introduces us into the eternal happiness of Heaven. Grace is like a seed that blossoms into the eternal life of Heaven.

67. How can we acquire grace?

God gives us grace through Baptism. If a person loses it by committing mortal sin, he can get it back through the Sacrament of Penance or Reconciliation, that is, confession.

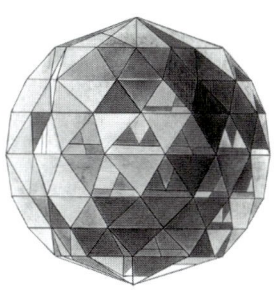

A soul in the state of grace is like a brilliant diamond.

The soul without grace is like a dull, dark diamond

68. What is mortal sin?

Mortal sin is serious disobedience to a commandment of God, done with full knowledge and consent of the will.

69. Which are the most frequent mortal sins?

The most frequent mortal sins are blasphemy, missing Mass on Sundays or holy days of obligation, disobedience to parents in serious matters, sins against the virtues of purity and chastity, and stealing valuable items.

70. What should a person do who has committed a mortal sin?

"As the Father has sent me, I also send you (...) Receive the Holy Spirit; whose sins you shall forgive, they are forgiven them; and whose sins you shall retain, they are retained" (Jn 20:21, 23).

A person who has committed a mortal sin should repent immediately, beg God's forgiveness, and try to go to confession as soon as possible. If a person commits even just one mortal sin, he may not receive Communion until he has been to confession.

71. **What happens if a person receives Holy Communion in mortal sin?**

A person who receives Holy Communion in mortal sin commits the grave sin of sacrilege.

72. **If grace is conferred by Baptism and confession and the person who receives the Eucharist must already be in the state of grace, how can the Eucharist confer grace?**

The Eucharist confers grace by increasing it. The Eucharist is food for the soul. Just as we need to eat to stay alive and grow, so to keep ourselves in the state of grace and grow in it we need to receive Communion often and worthily—not just often, but also worthily.

73. **Does the Eucharist have any other effects?**

The confessional

The Eucharist has many other wonderful effects, all related to an increase in grace. The Eucharist makes us one with Jesus since it unites us in intimate communion with Him, and as a consequence we are all made one: "Because the bread is one, we, though many, are one body, all of us who partake of the one bread," says Saint Paul (1 Cor 10:17). The Eucharist plants the seed of our future resurrection in us, uniting us with Jesus Christ who rose from the dead. Finally, it remits our venial sins as long as we are free of any attachment to them.

"'Rejoice with me, because I have found my sheep that was lost.' I say to you that, even so, there will be joy in heaven over one sinner who repents, more than over ninety-nine just who have no need of repentance" (Lk 15:6-7).

We can find God anywhere and anytime, but especially when we go into a Catholic church or chapel!

How to Receive Holy Communion Worthily

74. What should we do to receive Holy Communion worthily?

Three things are required : 1) to be in the grace of God; 2) to be conscious and aware of Whom we are going to receive; 3) to fast for at least one hour (except for water or medicine).

Jesus is truly present in the consecrated Host

75. What does it mean to be conscious and aware of Whom we are going to receive?

In the first place it means that we know the fundamental truths about the Eucharist, but most of all it means that we are aware that Jesus is truly living and present in the consecrated Host. When we receive Holy Communion we should rekindle our faith in order to receive Jesus fervently, devoutly, and lovingly. Only in this way can Holy Communion yield its full fruit. This is what it means to be conscious and aware of Whom we are going to receive.

Holy Communion can be received directly on the tongue or in the hand

How should we receive Holy Communion?

Holy Communion can be received by letting the priest place the Sacred Host directly on the tongue. If we wish we can also receive It in the hand, if we know how to do it properly. We must place the open palm of our left hand on top of our right hand, so that the priest can place the Sacred Host in it; then we must immediately and respectfully take the Host by the thumb and forefinger of the right hand and reverently place It in our mouth. As we have already said, if we realize that any little pieces have remained in our hand, we must place them, too, in our mouth.

77. What should we do after receiving Holy Communion?

After receiving Holy Communion, aware that Jesus is truly present within us, we should recollect ourselves in profound prayer. If there is a hymn instead of a period of silence for everyone, we should spend some time in silence after the final blessing.

St. Catherine of Siena, after receiving Holy Communion, would fall into ecstasy and no one could move her from her place. We should not forget that Jesus is truly present within us for as long as the Eucharistic species last, that is, for about a quarter of an hour.

78. **Are these moments of prayer after Holy Communion important?**

They are very important, even though, unfortunately, most people neglect them these days. And yet, if we think about how we have the real and living Jesus within us, how can we not feel the need to be deeply absorbed in prayer?

Thanksgiving after
Holy Communion

79. **How should we spend the time when Jesus is still physically present within us?**

The important thing is to remain recollected and not to be distracted by things like unnecessary talking. We can read a prayer book, or, if we are able, we can use our own words to talk to Jesus, who is present in our heart.

We can recall the word ACTS, which reminds us that we should make acts of Adoration, Contrition, Thanksgiving, and Supplication (petition).

Eucharistic Adoration: we are truly in the presence of Jesus!

Is our devotion to Jesus, present in the Holy Eucharist, restricted to a few minutes after Communion?

There is another very beautiful way to show our love for Jesus in the Eucharist and to receive many graces from Him. It is called Eucharistic adoration, which we do by praying silently in front of the tabernacle, or more solemnly by participating in public adoration when the Blessed Sacrament is exposed in the monstrance.

Eucharistic adoration is a very expressive sign of our faith in Jesus' Real Presence and allows us to meet Him as the people of Palestine did in His time.

We are no less fortunate than they; rather, in a sense, we are even more fortunate than they were, because we can find Jesus Our Lord anywhere, anytime by simply going into a Catholic church or chapel. Jesus is there for us, ready to listen to us, to grant all our requests, to comfort us in our afflictions and to help us in our troubles.

If only we had a little more faith and love, there would never be an empty church because there would always be someone kneeling before the tabernacle.

"Let the children come to me...for to such belongs the kingdom of heaven" (Mt 19:14).

PART TWO

EUCHARISTIC MIRACLES

(By the
Institute of St. Clement I,
Pope and Martyr)

Eucharistic miracles can be linked to Jesus' Birth. Just as the divinity of Christ was hidden under the humble appearances of a baby laid in a manger, so are the Body and Blood of Jesus hidden under the species of bread and wine. It is very significant that the word "Bethlehem" means "house of bread," and Jesus says: "I am the bread of life" (Jn 6:48).

Father Daniel the Faranite's Story
From the Acts of the Desert Fathers
(third through fifth centuries)

Father Daniel the Faranite once told the following story: "Father Arsenius once told us of a very industrious monk of Skete who did not know much about the faith. Because of his ignorance, he mistakenly said one day: 'The bread we eat is not really the Body of Christ, but a symbol.' Two elderly monks, hearing his words and knowing that he was a good and pious man, supposed that he was talking that way not on purpose but only through ignorance. They went to him and said: 'Father, we heard someone saying something against the faith: that the bread we receive is not the true Body of Christ, but a symbol.' And the old Father answered: 'I'm the one who says that!'

"The two elderly monks then started to exhort him: 'You mustn't believe that; you must believe what the Catholic Church has handed down to us. We believe that this bread is the Body of Christ and this chalice is the Blood of Christ, in reality and not symbolically.' (....) 'The old Father answered: 'Unless something happens to convince me otherwise, I won't believe it.' The two monks said: 'This week we will pray about this mystery and we believe that God will reveal it to us.' (....)

"At the end of the week, on Sunday, they went to church and all three stood together, the old Father on a step between the other two. Their eyes were opened. When the bread for the sacrifice was placed on the altar, the

three of them, and only they, saw a child instead of the bread. When the priest reached out to break the bread, there came from Heaven an angel of God holding a sword. He sacrificed the child and poured his blood into the chalice. When the priest broke the bread into pieces, the angel of God cut pieces of flesh from the child; when the monks approached the altar to receive the holy gifts, the old Father received bleeding flesh. The sight frightened him and he cried: 'I believe, O Lord, that the bread is your Body and the chalice is your Blood.' And immediately the flesh he was holding in his hand took on the appearances of bread, according to the mystery; and he received Holy Communion with gratitude to God."

2. The Host Changes Into Bleeding Flesh
Rome (sixth or seventh century)

This miracle happened on a Sunday, while Pope St. Gregory the Great was celebrating Mass in St. Peter's Basilica.

At Communion time a Roman noblewoman approached the altar. The Pope, placing the Host on her lips, pronounced the ritual words: "May the Body of Our Lord Jesus Christ serve for the remission of your sins and lead you to eternal life." An incredulous expression of amusement passed over the woman's face. Noticing this, St. Gregory the Great took the Host back and gave it to the deacon to put on the altar until after Communion.

When the ceremony was finished, the Pope turned to the woman and said: "Tell me, I beg you, what were you thinking when you laughed as you were about to receive Holy Communion?" The woman said: "Wasn't the bread you were going to give me the same bread I myself baked and brought for the offering? I couldn't help smiling when you called the bread that I kneaded with my own hands the Body of Christ."

The Pope invited all the faithful to pray and ask God that the woman might not persist in her unbelief. Then he returned to the altar. At that moment, to the indescribable emotion of those present, the Eucharistic veils covering the Sacred Host disappeared, and everybody could see that the bread had changed into the bleeding flesh of Christ.

When the skeptical woman had seen the true presence of the Body of Christ, the Host again took on the form of bread, with the exception of a tiny part which remained blood-stained and is now kept in Bavaria, in the village of Andechs.

3. The Miracle of Lanciano, Italy (750)

At Lanciano, in Italy, around 750, Jesus wanted to give a proof of His Real Presence in the Eucharist.

In St. Francis' Church, where the miracle took place, a marble plaque tells of the prodigy of which the relics are still preserved: "In the year of Our Lord about 700,

in this church, a monk doubted that in the consecrated Host there was truly the Body of Our Lord and in the chalice, His Blood. He celebrated Mass and, after pronouncing the words of consecration, he saw the Host change into flesh and the wine into blood. The miracle was shown to those present and to the whole people.

"The flesh is still one piece and the blood is divided into five unequal parts which all together weigh the same as each one individually.

"All this can be seen in this chapel built by John Francis Valsecca, at his own expense, in the Year of the Lord 1636."

The laboratory tests, done several times and by different experts in recent years, confirm that this is human flesh and human blood, which are preserved incorrupt.

The monstrance of Lanciano

4. The Miracle of Ferrara, Italy (1171)

The traces of the miracle of the blood which gushed out of the Host on Easter Sunday, March 28, 1171, are kept in the Basilica of St. Mary-in-Vado in Ferrara.

During Mass, blood gushed out of the broken Host and stained the vault above the altar. Some witnesses said they also saw the Host assuming a blood-red color. Other witnesses said they saw the figure of a child in place of the Host.

The traces of blood on the vault above the altar are indisputable, however, as we can still observe today in the Basilica of St. Mary-in-Vado in Ferrara.

5. The Miracle of St. Anthony of Padua (1227)

St. Anthony was involved in a dispute with heretics who denied the Real Presence of Jesus in the Eucharist. They asked to see an undeniable proof, and he promised them a miracle.

One heretic, named Bonovillo, said: "I have a mule which I will keep locked up without food for three days. After the three days I will bring her to the main square

of the town, in front of all the people, and there I will give her fodder; you will bring the Host which, as you say, contains the Body of the Man-God. If the mule refuses the oats and kneels down in front of the Host, I'll become a Catholic."

St. Anthony retired to his monastery and for three days addressed himself to the Lord, praying and fasting.

On the appointed day he arrived with the Blessed Sacrament. As the saint approached, a deep silence fell over the crowd. St. Anthony, in a loud, firm voice, said to the animal: "In the name of your Creator, whom I, though unworthy, hold living, true, real, and substantial in my hands, I order you, irrational pack animal, to come here at once and prostrate in front of Him, so that the heretics might recognize that all creatures are subject and obedient to the Lamb of God Whom we sacrifice on our altars."

The heretic was in a cold sweat, shouting at the animal and tempting her with the food she was so hungry for. The animal, however, refused her master's food and obediently approached St. Anthony. She bent her forelegs in front of the Host and remained in that position.

Anthony was not mistaken in judging the loyalty of his rival. The heretic fell at St. Anthony's feet, publicly abjuring his errors, and from that day on became one of the saint's most zealous cooperators. His whole family also entered the true Church, and, in the ardor of his gratitude to God, with his own means he built a church dedicated to St. Peter, Prince of the Apostles.

6. The Miracle of Alatri, Italy (1228)

In the town of Alatri, in the Basilica of St. Paul the Apostle, the relic of the Eucharistic miracle known as the "miracle of the incarnated Host," which took place in 1228, is still kept today.

The story of this prodigious event has been handed down to us by an authoritative document, the papal bull of Gregory IX, *Fraternitas tuae,* dated March 13, 1228:

The monstrance kept in Alatri

"Gregory, Bishop and servant of the servants of God, to our venerable brother Bishop of Alatri, health and apostolic benediction. We have received your letter, dearest brother, which informed us of how a young lady, strongly influenced by the bad advice of a wicked woman, after receiving the Most Sacred Body of Christ from the hands of the priest, kept It in her mouth until, at an opportune moment, she could hide It in a towel where, three days later, she found the same Body, which she had received under the species of bread, changed into flesh, as everyone can still see with his own eyes today."

The Miracle of St. Clare of Assisi (1240)

The Saracens laid siege to Assisi and even broke into the cloister at San Damiano, the monastery where St. Clare and the other nuns lived.

At that sight, the nuns' hearts sank; terrified, they hurried to call Clare. Prostrating herself in prayer, she implored Christ, saying to Him: "My Lord, do you want to hand over your defenseless servants, whom I have brought up for love of you, to the pagans? I implore you, Lord, protect these your servants, whom I alone cannot save."

Suddenly a child's voice, coming from the monstrance, sounded in her ears: "I shall always protect you!" "My Lord," added St. Clare, "if it please you, protect also this town, which supports us for love of you." And Christ said to her: "This town shall have to undergo many sufferings, but it shall be defended by my protection."

The virgin then raised her face, bathed in tears, and consoled the weeping nuns: "I promise you, my daughters, that nothing will hurt you; you must only have faith in Christ!"

With a fearless heart, Clare, though she was ill, had herself carried face to face with the enemy, holding in her hand the ivory monstrance containing the consecrated Host.

The Saracens miraculously fled, and the town of Assisi was spared.

8. The Miracle of Bolsena, Italy (1263)

The Eucharistic miracle of the blood-stained corporal, which is kept in the cathedral of Orvieto, took place in St. Christina's Church in Bolsena, in 1263.

These words are inscribed on the memorial stone in Bolsena: "At the time when Pope Urban I, of happy memory, together with his brother cardinals and his Curia, resided in Orvieto, there was a German priest, of uncommon prudence and outstanding morals, who in everything showed himself faithful to God, though much doubting in faith in the Sacrament of the Eucharist. How could it be that, at the words uttered by the priest, 'This is my Body,' the bread would change into the real and most sacred Body of Christ, and by his uttering the other words, 'This is my Blood,' the wine would change into Blood?

"Upon his arrival at the castle of Bolsena, he decided to celebrate Mass in this Church of St. Christina the Virgin. (...) During the celebration, while he was holding the Host in his hands over the chalice, such a marvelous event took place, that its miracle has been a source of astonishment both in the past and in the present. Suddenly the Host appeared, in a visible manner, as true blood-stained flesh, except for that part which he held in his fingers. Moreover, a cloth which was used to purify the chalice was stained by the effusion of blood. At the sight of the miracle, he who formerly doubted was confirmed in his faith and, astonished, decided to conceal everything with the corporal (...).

"The drops of blood which welled up, staining the corporal, left engraved as many identical figures of a man [as there were drops of blood]. Seeing this, the terrified priest stopped celebrating Mass, not daring to proceed. Instead, seized by deep sorrow and repentance, he first put the venerable Sacrament with due reverence and devotion in the church's tabernacle, then hurried to the Supreme Pontiff himself and, kneeling before him, told him all that had happened and of his hardness of heart, begging for forgiveness and mercy.

"The Pope listened to the story and, full of the greatest admiration, absolved the priest, imposing on him a salutary penance.

"The Pontiff, taking the venerable Sacrament in his hands and genuflecting, brought it to the church in Orvieto with hymns and songs, with great joy and rejoicing, and solemnly placed it in the tabernacle. It

Corpus Christi Procession

was the Year of the Nativity of Our Lord Jesus Christ, 1263."

That was the first Corpus Christi procession. The same Urban IV established the feast of Corpus Christi the following year, 1264.

9. The Miracle of Bagno di Romagna, Italy (1412)

In 1412, Father Lazzaro of Venice was prior of the Camaldolese monastery. One day while celebrating Mass in St. Mary's Church in Bagno, at the moment of the Consecration, he started thinking of the great mysteries and was assailed by a common temptation: he began to wonder whether, under the consecrated species, the real and living Jesus Christ, with His Body, Blood, Soul and Divinity, were truly present.

Suddenly the consecrated wine in the chalice lost the appearance of wine and changed into blood. Bubbling up as though it were

The consecrated wine starts to foam and changes into Blood

alive, it rose to the edge of the chalice and overflowed, staining the corporal.

His eyes full of tears, the prior proclaimed that this miracle, an incontestable proof of the Real Presence of Jesus in the Sacrament of the Altar, was willed by God's mercy in order to dissipate doubts and temptations.

This miraculous corporal is still kept in St. Mary's Church in Bagno and is greatly venerated by the faithful, who every year on Corpus Christi Sunday carry it in procession through the village.

10. The Miracle of Turin, Italy (1453)

The thief steals the monstrance containing the Sacred Host

Among all Eucharistic miracles, one of the most famous is the one which took place in Turin on June 6th, 1453, during the sack of foreign soldiers on their way to the Piedmontese city.

One of these wicked soldiers went to a church in the village of Exilles, broke into the tabernacle and took the silver monstrance containing the consecrated Host. He wrapped it in a cloth, put it in a sack together with his other loot, and loaded it all on the back of his mule.

When they arrived in Turin, the mule stopped in front of St. Sylvester's Church and refused to go on, in spite of his master's blows.

People tried in vain to get the poor animal, who seemed petrified, to move. Suddenly, without anyone's touch-

The mule refuses to budge, and the monstrance
miraculously rises into the air

ing it, the sack containing the loot started to move as
if it were alive. The cords around it broke, and the
monstrance with the consecrated Host fell out. Nobody
dared to touch it, so filled with horror were they at the
sacrilege which had been committed.

The monstrance rose and hovered in the air, high
enough so that everybody in the square could see it.
There it remained, motionless, as if held by an invisible hand. A bright ray of light emanated from the
Sacred Host.

The wicked soldier was astonished, and all the people
fell to their knees, praying, weeping, beating their
breasts, and pleading for mercy.

News of the miracle spread like lightning. Among the
crowd that rushed to the scene was the Bishop of the
city, Msgr. Louis Romagnono, who was the protago-
nist of the second part of the miracle: the monstrance

opened, showing the miraculous Host which shone like the midday sun. The Bishop ordered a chalice to be brought and raised it towards the Host, tearfully imploring the Blessed Sacrament to descend and remain with His children. At this prayer the light faded and the Sacred Host went to settle in the chalice held by the Bishop, leaving behind a bright trail which disappeared immediately.

The Bishop's prayers bring the monstrance down

Then a solemn procession took place. Amidst prayers and hymns of joy, the miraculous Host was placed in the city's cathedral. On the spot where the miracle happened, the Church of Corpus Domini was erected as a perpetual memorial. It is one of Turin's most important churches, and a plaque still reminds us of the event today.

11. The Miracle of Siena, Italy (1730)

The thieves steal the Hosts

The day before Siena's famous horse race in 1730, some thieves broke into the Friars Minor Church at the Camollia Gate, raided the tabernacle and stole the consecrated Hosts. The Hosts were found two days later in the poor box of another church, St. Mary of Provenzano, by a cleric who collected the offerings.

They were the same 351 stolen Hosts. To make sure, they were checked against the mold used to prepare them. They fit perfectly! Once cleaned, the Hosts were carefully preserved but nearly forgotten.

Almost half a century passed and, on the occasion of a provincial chapter, the Minister General of the Friars Minor, Father Vipera, visited the monastery of Siena. He heard the story of the Hosts and wanted to see them. They were amazingly intact.

People started to talk of a miracle. In 1789 the Bishop of Siena ordered an investigation: 320 Hosts were as fresh as if they had just been made, while the others were damaged only because of being handled in the investigation.

The Hosts remain intact for nearly 300 years

Still uncertain, the Bishop decided on a further test: he ordered a certain number of unconsecrated hosts placed in a container similar to the one containing the stolen Hosts, to be opened ten years later. Only decomposed fragments and worms came out!

In 1914 Bishop Scaccia submitted the Hosts for examination to a group of chemists (among them the Servant of God Joseph Toniolo), who verified their perfect state. The Hosts, which had been made with unleavened bread, still tasted perfectly good.

On September 14, 1980, John Paul II knelt in front of the urn and said: "It is the presence of God!" Even today, after nearly 300 years, the miraculous Hosts remain intact in St. Francis' Church in Siena.

12. The Eucharist and Our Lady of Lourdes, France (1888)

St. Bernadette

In Lourdes, thirty years after the apparitions of Our Lady to St. Bernadette (who was deeply devoted to the Eucharist), on August 22, 1888, a French priest taking part in the National Pilgrimage suggested having a procession with the Blessed Sacrament.

At four o'clock that day, the sick, together with the pilgrims, were blessed in front of the cave of the apparition for the first time. What a sight! There is no more beautiful act of faith in the Real Presence of Jesus in Eucharist than the one that takes place in Lourdes during the procession and blessing of the sick with the Blessed Sacrament.

At that first procession there was a sudden and very important healing: a gentleman named Pierre Delannoy, who had suffered for years from ataxia (an inability to coordinate voluntary muscular movements, an illness which inevitably leads to death), was instantaneously healed when the monstrance containing the Blessed Sacrament passed in front of him. It was the first Eucharistic miracle to take place at Lourdes.

The miraculous healing of Pierre Delannoy at the
blessing with the Blessed Sacrament

Since August 22, 1888, the Eucharistic procession for
the sick has never been omitted. This is why the shrine
of Lourdes has become one of the most evident testi-
monies of faith in the Real Presence of Jesus in the
Eucharist.

13. The Healing of Marie Louise Horeau (1889)

In 1889, a completely blind young woman, Marie Louise Horeau, asked to be taken to Lourdes by train on the National Pilgrimage. Full of trust, she had herself immersed twice in the miraculous waters, but nothing happened. On the second day at about four o'clock, during Benediction of the Blessed Sacrament, she was praying on her knees by the cave. After Benediction, the procession moved towards the Basilica.

All the sick were there, lying on their beds, looking to the Lord, who was about to pass among them, for comfort or healing; a huge crowd knelt around them. There were acclamations on all sides. Marie Louise couldn't approach the cave, so she had to wait by the pool. Her heart was ready.

There, full of trust, she awaited the approach of the Good Master; she asked the friend who was leading and guiding her to let her know the exact moment when Our Lord would be near: "When the Blessed Sacrament comes this way," she said, "please tell me! I want to acclaim Him and address my fervent prayers to Him."

When Jesus was about to pass near Marie Louise, her friend whispered quickly in her ear: "Here He comes!"

The poor woman fell to her knees and with ineffable faith started to cry out: "Hosanna, hosanna to the Son of God! Oh Good Master, have mercy on me! My Lord, let me see!"

At that very moment, a dazzling light passed before her eyes and at the same time a stabbing pain shot

The miraculous healing of Marie Louise Horeau who regained her sight

through her: her eyes were opened. She began to see the Sacred Host, the Bishop holding the monstrance, and the crowd all around her. Far away she could see the cave from which the white statue of Our Lady seemed to smile at her! Marie Louise Horeau was completely healed at the passing of the Blessed Sacrament.

14. The Healing of Gabriel Gargam (1899)

Gabriel Gargam was a postal worker. On December 17, 1899, at 10:30 PM, while on duty on a train leaving from Bordeaux, he was involved in a railway accident.

The terrible crash threw Gabriel about ten yards down a slope, right into the snow. He was found rigid, without the least sign of life, only towards 7:00 the next morning. That frightful crash proved such a shock to his system that none of his members was functioning.

Two years later gangrene set in in his feet, a sure sign of approaching death. Hearing of the pilgrimage to Lourdes, Gabriel Gargam asked to be registered, moved not by his faith but by his desire to leave the hospital.

Arriving in Lourdes when the procession of the Blessed Sacrament had already started, he was laid on the ground more dead than alive. After a few minutes he fell into a coma. Suddenly, while the golden monstrance containing Jesus in the Eucharist approached him, miraculously he stood up and started to walk behind the Blessed Sacrament, completely healed.

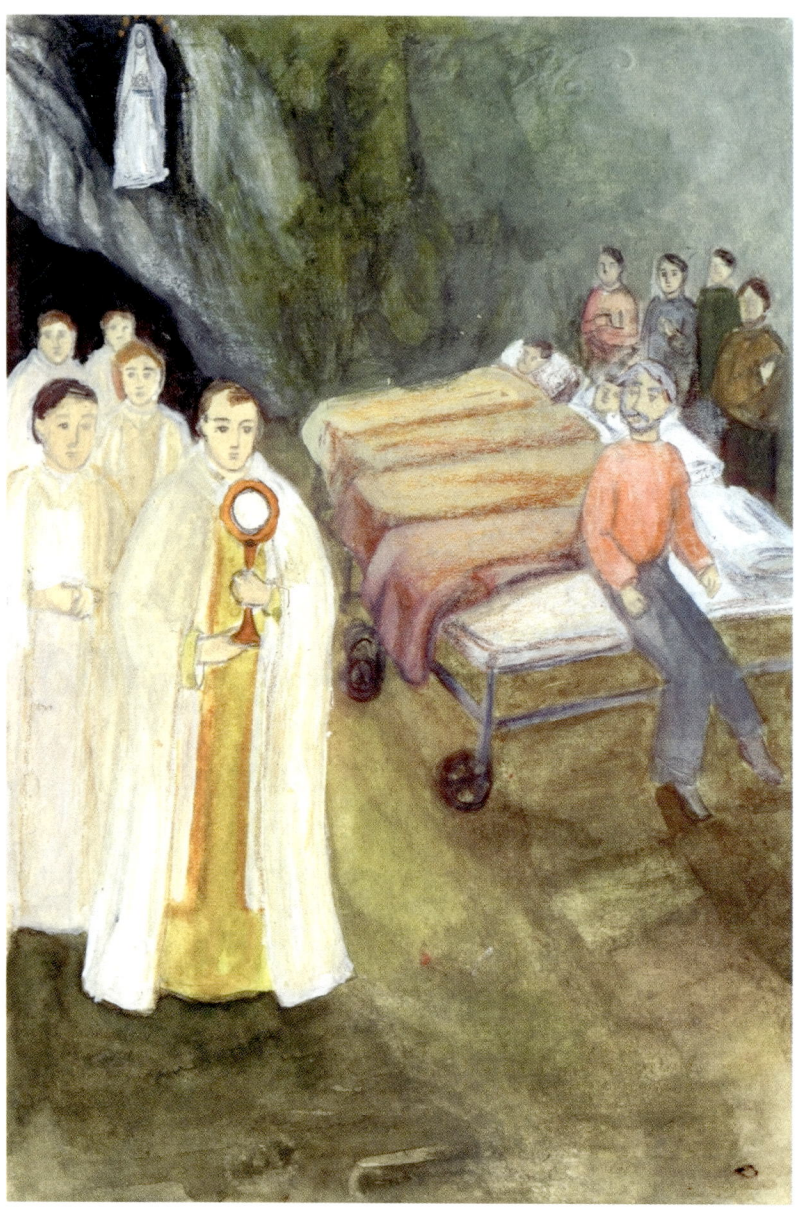

Gabriel Gargam miraculously walks again

15. The Face Etched on the Host at Saint-André de la Réunion (1902)

The Eucharistic prodigy of St. Andrew's Parish on the island of La Réunion—a beautiful African island in the Indian Ocean—took place on January 26, 1902. The island was a French colony at the time.

Abbot Lacombe, the church's parish priest, witnessed the miracle, which he himself recounted to thousands of people at the Eucharistic Congress in Angoulême (1904) as well as to a group of priests at a retreat in the town of Périgueux.

It was the Sunday before Lent. Abbot Lacombe exposed the Eucharist before the High Mass, which was usually attended by nearly all the faithful of the parish (the place was 27 km from the capital, Saint-Denis).

While the choir was singing the *Sanctus,* the priest raised his glance towards the Host and saw something that made him stop, amazed and dumbfounded, and rub his eyes. Overcoming his emotions, he looked around to be sure that everything was as usual and finished Mass as if nothing had happened.

Once back in the sacristy, he met a parishioner who wanted to have his medal blessed. He sent the man to the altar and asked him to look carefully at the Host which was still exposed there.

The man returned immediately, very agitated, his hands clasped, claiming to have seen on the Host the sorrowful face of a man with his eyes closed, his head inclined to the right, his cheeks streaming with tears. "It's unbelievable!" he burst out. Abbot Lacombe began to tremble. The man had seen the same thing! He called two altar boys and went back to the altar. On the Host there was still the image in relief of the suffering face, a very lifelike image that was pressed against the glass of the monstrance.

Only two women and a child were still in the church. The women were asked to come up, and they confirmed the same vision. So did the child. Meanwhile the altar boys ran out of the church shouting the news of the miracle.

The faithful of the parish came back to the church in droves. Some people arrived from the capital bringing binoculars with them, but they immediately put them back in their cases because the vision, which was clear and bright, could be seen with the naked eye.

The face of Jesus appears in the Host

The abbot was scrupulously careful and used every precaution. Fearing that it could be the effect of a reflection, he had all the candles extinguished and the windows shut. The phenomenon appeared even brighter. In fact, in the darkness actual flashes of light emanated from the face.

In the early afternoon the image changed. Instead of the blood-stained face, a crucifix appeared, covering the whole Host from top to bottom. After Benediction, the vision disappeared.

The efficacy of the Eucharist is well symbolized by the bread the angel brought to the prophet Elias. The strength of that bread sustained the prophet for forty days until he reached Mount Horeb.
The Eucharist is the miraculous Bread that Jesus gave us so we would have the necessary strength to reach Heaven.

PART THREE

THE SAINTS
AND THE EUCHARIST

(By the
Institute of St. Clement I,
Pope and Martyr)

All the saints were very devoted to the Eucharist, drawing from It their strength and love. The Virgin Mary, Queen of all Saints, is our heavenly Mother who guides us to worship and live the mystery of the God made man, hidden under the Eucharistic species of bread and wine.

1. St. Tarcisius, Martyr (third century)

The young Tarcisius generously and courageously offered to secretly bring the Eucharist to Christian prisoners during the persecutions.

Pope Damasus I tells us: "Tarcisius was carrying the mysteries of Christ when a criminal hand tried to profane them; he preferred to give his life rather than give the Body of the Lord to those wicked men."

St. Tarcisius prefers to die rather than give the consecrated Host to those who would profane It

2. St. Francis of Assisi (1181–1226)

St. Francis, founder of the Franciscan Order and patron of Italy, though he considered himself unworthy to receive Holy Orders, received the gift of the stigmata from Jesus on Mount Verna.

He greatly loved the Eucharist and the Church. He burned with love for the Sacrament of the Body of Christ and considered it a serious sign of contempt not to attend Mass daily. He received Communion often and with such devotion that he inflamed the devotion of others as well.

"Francis, rebuild my Church," the crucifix at the church of San Damiano told him one day. Francis became the rebuilder *par excellence*. Without complaining or condemning anyone, but with humility and evangelical poverty, Francis repaired church buildings, adorned them with sacred furnishings and vestments, swept the churchyards, decorated the altars, and honored priests more than angels.

Francis exhorts us in his writings: "The chalices, corporals, altar furnishings and everything else connected with the Holy Sacrifice must be precious. Everyone should praise and kneel before the Blessed Sacrament, in which is hidden the Lord God, living and true."

He also wanted great respect shown to the hands of the priest because the divine power to consecrate this sacrament has been conferred on them. He often said, "Were I to meet a saint coming from Heaven, like the deacon St. Lawrence, and a very poor priest at the same time, I would first greet the priest and run to kiss his hands. I would say: 'Wait, St. Lawrence, because the hands of this man touch the Word of life and have superhuman power.'"

Very significant are his words: "Behold, every day He humbles Himself (cf. Phil 2:8), just as when 'from royal thrones' (Wis 18:15) He came into the womb of the Virgin; every day He comes to us Himself humbly appearing; every day He descends from the bosom of the Father upon the altar in the hands of the priest. And just as to the holy Apostles in true flesh, so even now He shows Himself to us in the Sacred Bread. And just as when they gazed at His very own flesh they saw only His flesh, but contemplating with spiritual eyes believed Him to be God, so we too seeing bread and wine with bodily eyes, are to see and firmly believe, that they are His Most Holy Body and Blood, living and true. And in such a manner the Lord is always with His faithful, just as He Himself says: 'Behold I am with you even to the consummation of the age' (cf. Mt 28:20)."

St. Francis kisses the hands of the priest

3. St. Thomas Aquinas (1225-1274)

St. Thomas Aquinas is the Catholic Church's greatest theologian. He was very devoted to the Eucharist. In his times, in the 1200's, priests did not usually celebrate Mass every day. However, St. Thomas, when he was not prevented by some serious difficulty like an illness, used to celebrate Mass every day, and then, as an act of thanksgiving, he attended another Mass celebrated by one of his brothers in religion.

It is said that he was often moved to tears, and sometimes he could not go on celebrating Mass. One day, while celebrating Mass, he was so engrossed that some of those present approached him and tried to shake him out of his trance so he could finish his Mass. After Mass, they asked him what he had felt during those moments of intense prayer, but his only answer was: "I cannot talk about it." We know that the higher one's prayer is, the less possible it is to put it into words. There is a liturgical hymn, composed by St. Bernard, which speaks of this phenomenon: "The tongue cannot speak, the hand cannot write; only the one who has experienced it, knows what it is to love Jesus."

The great importance of the Eucharist in the life and thought of St. Thomas can be seen by the story of his last Communion. On that occasion the saint pronounced the following touching words, which reveal his inner striving and his passion as theologian and seeker: "I receive thee, price of my redemption, viaticum of my pilgrimage, for love of whom I have fasted, prayed, taught and labored. Never have I said a word against thee; if I have it was in ignorance and I do not persist in my ignorance. But if I have expressed myself badly regarding this sacrament or any other, I leave the correction of my work to the Holy Roman Church, and in that obedience I pass from this life."

We know that St. Thomas taught about all aspects of this sacrament extraordinarily well, because the Roman Catholic Church has made practically his entire Eucharistic doctrine her own. Many Councils have made use of his words to express Catholic doctrine and defend it against the errors of heretics.

St. Thomas is also known for having written the texts of the liturgical Office and the Mass of Corpus Christi. Very famous is the prayer he wrote as a thanksgiving after Holy Communion: "O sweetest Jesus, may your most sacred Body and Blood be sweetness and lightness to the soul, salvation and holiness against all temptations, joy and peace in every tribulation, light and strength in every word and action, and a sure help at the moment of death. Amen."

4. St. Catherine of Siena (1347-1380)

As a very young woman, St. Catherine entered the Dominican Order, becoming one of the most eminent figures of her time.

Pope Pius XII proclaimed her a co-patroness of Italy; Paul VI proclaimed her Doctor of the Church, and John Paul II declared her co-patroness of Europe.

Many passages about the Eucharist can be found in the book she wrote under divine inspiration, the *Dialogue*. In one of the most famous passages of this treatise, Jesus said to the saint: "Think, my dearest daughter, what a most excellent state the soul reaches when it properly receives the bread of life, nourishment of angels. In receiving it, the soul is in me and I in it; just as the fish is in the sea and the sea is in the fish, so I am in the soul and the soul is in me, the sea of peace. Grace remains in the soul, and it remains because the soul has received the bread of life in the state of grace; after the species of bread is consumed, I leave behind the imprint of my grace, like a seal pressed on warm wax: when the seal is removed, the mark remains."

5. North American Martyrs (1648–1649)

Isaac Jogues, Jean de la Lande, Jean de Brébeuf, Gabriel Lalemant, Antoine Daniel, Charles Garnier, Noel Chabanel and René Goupil were all Jesuit priests who were very devoted to the Eucharist and wanted to bring love for the Most Holy Sacrament to all who had not had the privilege of knowing this great treasure. They chose to consecrate their lives to the evangelization of the natives in the vast and then-unexplored lands of North America around the border between Canada and the United States, lands with huge forests and lakes as big as seas.

It was devotion to the Holy Eucharist above all that gave these Jesuits the necessary strength in all their difficulties. "Our weapons are the sacraments," they said. Fr. Buteux wrote of his edification when he saw St. Isaac Jogues "like a soul glued, so to speak, to the Blessed Sacrament." St. Charles Garnier exclaimed: "The Eucharist is the source of all sweetness and the support of our heart... It seems as if God, supplying for what we lack, and as a reward, has taken up His residence in these poor cabins; He wants to shower us with blessings." In those poor huts, Jesus in the Host was a comfort to all of them.

It was before the tabernacle that this holy missionary received many mystical graces: "O my dear brother," wrote Charles Garnier, "bless God because He has given me brothers who are martyrs and saints who aspire to that crown each day. From now on I regard myself as a Host which is to be immolated."

The missionaries had their first successes with the nearest and most sociable of the Hurons, but in 1640 the Hurons were attacked by a tribe of Iroquois, known as the most warlike and ferocious of tribes. A real war of extermination began between these two groups. Before it was over, the eight French Jesuits were put to death. We will not recount their story nor their excruciating sufferings here. Suffice it to say that these sufferings were extreme since the Iroquois were particularly cruel in torturing their enemies for hours and even days before their deaths.

Thanks to the sacrifice of these martyrs, Christianity spread throughout the regions of North America. In the decades after their death, the Catholic settlement grew strong with new and fruitful works.

St. Gaspar del Bufalo (1786-1837)

St. Gaspar, founder of the Missionaries of the Most Precious Blood, was passionately engaged in preaching and assisting the poor.

He did all he could to spread devotion to the Precious Blood of Jesus and to the Holy Eucharist. He urged all to love the Blood Jesus shed to redeem us.

St. Gaspar says in his writings: "The Eucharist fortifies us and gives us strength. St. Thomas says that one of the reasons why this Most Holy Sacrament defends us and frees us from temptations is because, since it is the memorial of Christ's sufferings through which the demons were defeated, they flee as soon as they see Jesus' Body and Blood within us."

He also said: "O my Jesus, when I think of you humiliated under the Eucharistic species, I am moved and deeply touched! The love of a God," he exclaimed, "has gone to such lengths!"

He visited the Blessed Sacrament every day and remained there for hours. The Eucharist was for him the center of life, the beginning and the end of every path to holiness.

7. St. John Neumann (1811–1860)

St. John Neumann was born in Bohemia and studied there for the priesthood. He was very talented and learned many languages. Hearing that there were Catholic immigrants with no priests in the new country called the United States, he set sail for America. In 1836 he was ordained a priest in New York City.

Fr. John worked very hard with the immigrants from many countries, including Ireland, Italy, and Germany. He was very concerned that the children should have Catholic schools, so he started the first Catholic school system in this country and founded a religious order of teachers. He also taught classes himself. Later he became a Redemptorist priest and then was made the bishop of Philadelphia, Pennsylvania.

The Blessed Sacrament was the great love of Bishop Neumann's life. He wrote, "I have only one desire, that of being near You in the Blessed Sacrament.... My Jesus, my love, my all, gladly would I endure hunger, thirst, heat and cold to remain always with You in the Blessed Sacrament."

Bishop Neumann wanted the parishes in his diocese to take turns having the Blessed Sacrament exposed in the monstrance for 40-hour periods. This is called the Forty Hours Devotion.

But some people in Philadelphia at that time were very anti-Catholic. Two churches had been burned down, and some priests told Bishop Neumann that it would be dangerous to hold the Forty Hours Devotion.

However, as the saintly bishop pondered and prayed over his problem, a strange event occurred. He fell asleep one night while writing at his desk and accidentally knocked over a candle. The flames burned all Bishop Neumann's letters except one—a letter he had written about the Forty Hours. As he knelt to thank God that he was still alive, he heard a voice telling him to go ahead and fear nothing.

Bishop Neumann immediately put his plan into action. The devotion was very successful and spread into other dioceses. Today Perpetual Eucharistic Adoration is spreading all across the United States.

8. St. John Bosco (1815-1888)

This holy priest was the founder of the Salesians and the Daughters of Mary Help of Christians. He dedicated himself with great fervor to the education of youth, founding oratories, schools and missions all over the world.

St. John Bosco was very devoted to the Eucharist. He had a deep faith in the Mass. He made it a rule for all his followers to attend daily Mass, and to all others he advised this practice, reminding them of St. Augustine, who said that one who would assiduously and devoutly attend Mass would not die in sin.

He also said that Our Lord listens in a special way to the prayers offered at the elevation of the sacramental species.

To all he said: "Do you want God to grant you many graces? Visit Him often. My dear friends! Visiting the Blessed Sacrament is a very necessary means of conquering the devil. Go to visit Jesus often, then, and the devil will not defeat you." He also said: "We must remember that this Sacrament is not only the memorial of what Jesus did, but it is also a sacrament by which mankind receives the same Body and Blood that Jesus sacrificed on the cross."

St. John Bosco miraculously multiplies the Hosts

9. St. Dominic Savio (1842–1857)

This young boy from the region of Piedmont in Italy was St. John Bosco's favorite student.

In those days children under twelve were not admitted to Holy Communion, but Dominic's Eucharistic piety was already so advanced that by an exceptional privilege, he received his First Communion when he was seven.

The day before his First Communion, St. Dominic wrote the following resolutions: "1. I will go to confession frequently and receive Holy Communion as often as my confessor allows; 2. I want to attend Mass on Sundays and holy days; 3. My friends will be Jesus and Mary; 4. Death rather than sin."

In the morning, before going to school, he would stop in front of the closed doors of the church, and on his knees he would pray to Jesus in the Eucharist. He had a cheerful character, but he was so fond of mortification that Don Bosco had to restrain him, telling him to give more importance to his daily duties and to games.

One day as the young saint genuflected before the Blessed Sacrament being carried to the sick by a priest, he saw a soldier standing next to him who did not genuflect. The young boy took his clean handkerchief out of his pocket and laid it in front of the soldier, who took the hint.

10. Blessed Bartolo Longo (1841-1926)

A brilliant lawyer, Bartolo dedicated himself to the building of the Shrine of Our Lady of Pompei and to catechizing the people of the area.

He was especially interested in the children, founding orphanages, nursery schools, homes for prisoners' children, and evening catechism classes and trade schools.

He was very devoted to the Holy

Eucharist. "What is my secret?" he asked. "Look there, to that tabernacle where the marble and gold shine brightly: there is His throne, His royal palace; in that ciborium, in that monstrance on the altar, there is Jesus, living and real, in His most august Mystery."

"At this most pure font I quenched the thirst of my children (....) I can prove this by the facts: Holy Communion with Christ is the most powerful means of educating children. Even the most incorrigible children born into criminal families can be transformed into angels by means of Holy Communion."

11. St. Katharine Drexel (1858-1955)

Katharine Drexel was born into a wealthy family who were very generous to the poor and outcast. She inherited a large sum of money from her parents. Katharine decided to use her money to help the Native Americans and African Americans who lived in extreme poverty and hardship.

While on a trip to Rome, Katharine asked the Holy Father, Pope Leo XIII, to send missionaries to these poor people. The Holy Father suggested that she become a missionary herself. Surprised, Katharine asked her spiritual director's advice. He recommended that she start a new religious order for women.

Katharine wanted to spend her life in adoration of the Blessed Sacrament, and she named her new order the Sisters of the Blessed Sacrament. These Sisters were to bring the Native Americans and African Americans to Christianity and thus to Christ in the Eucharist.

Everything Mother Katharine did began and ended before Jesus present on the altar. In the Eucharist she found the inspiration to fearlessly combat the terrible effects of racism and prejudice. Her prayer before the Lord led her to give herself entirely in the service of the poorest and most despised of His brothers and sisters.

"The spirit of the Eucharist consists in the donation of one's own being.... Get up after receiving Holy Communion and go find Him in the people.... Everything you do for the people, you do to Him," she wrote.

Mother Katharine led an extremely busy life, founding a missionary center, schools and universities, until in 1935 she suffered a heart attack. From that time until her holy death 20 years later, she spent much of her time in prayer before the Blessed Sacrament.

12. St. Gemma Galgani (1878-1903)

Gemma was an extraordinary saint, a mystic and a contemplative. From the time she was a child she wrote down her thoughts, her daily prayers, and her resolutions to live an ever purer life.

She used to speak with her guardian angel, assigning him delicate tasks like bringing to Rome the letters she

wrote to her spiritual father; the letters mysteriously arrived at their destination without the aid of the postal service.

She received the extraordinary gift of the stigmata. But above all, Gemma was deeply devoted to the Eucharist which was the center of her spirituality.

In spite of her illnesses she wanted to go to Mass every day; she often said, "It is most painful for me to stay away from Jesus in the Eucharist."

Gemma's day was divided between her prayers of thanksgiving for the Eucharist received that morning and prayers of preparation for the Communion to be received the following day.

13. St. Padre Pio of Pietrelcina (1887-1968)

Padre Pio is a saint of our times and is therefore very well-known. A great miracle worker and mystic, very devoted to the Eucharist and to Our Lady, he recommended the Rosary and considered the Mass the reference point of his spiritual life.

During one of his many ecstasies, Jesus said to Padre Pio: "With how much ingratitude is my love for man repaid (...)! They leave me alone in the churches at night, alone during the day. No one takes care of the Sacrament of the Altar any more; they never talk about this Sacrament of Love, and those who do talk about it, alas, with what indifference, with what coldness!"

In his teachings, Padre Pio insisted: "The Eucharist is the greatest of miracles; it is the utmost and greatest sign of Jesus' love for us. He did all this to give us a full, abundant, perfect life."

Padre Pio recommended the Eucharist as a means to reach holiness, as long as it is received with faith and purity of heart.

14. Blesseds Francisco and Jacinta Marto (The apparitions of Our Lady of Fatima, Portugal, 1917)

Around the ages of eight and six respectively, Francisco and Jacinta started to take their father's little flock to graze. While caring for the sheep, they usually joined their flock with their uncle's flock, taken to pasture by their cousin Lucia, who was a little older.

Francisco, Jacinta and Lucia during the apparition of the Angel of Eucharist

The three children would spend nearly the whole day outdoors watching the sheep. It was while tending their little flock that, in the autumn of 1916, the three children had an extraordinary encounter with the Angel of the Eucharist.

As Lucia said later, on that occasion an angel appeared to them; he was holding a chalice in his left hand while with his right hand he held over it a Host from which drops of blood fell into the chalice.

Our Lady appears to the three young shepherds

The angel knelt beside the three children, inviting them to repeat three times the following prayer: "Most Holy Trinity, Father, Son and Holy Spirit, I adore You profoundly and I offer You the most precious Body, Blood, Soul and Divinity of Our Lord Jesus Christ, present in all the tabernacles of the world, in reparation for the outrages, sacrileges and indifferences by which He is offended. By the infinite merits of the Sacred Heart of Jesus and the Immaculate Heart of Mary, I beg of you the conversion of poor sinners."

After having raised the chalice and the Host, the angel gave the Host to Lucia and invited Jacinta and Francisco to drink the contents of the chalice.

As he did so he said: "Take and drink the Body and the Blood of Jesus Christ, horribly outraged by ungrateful mankind. Make reparation for their crimes and console your God."

Prostrating once again, he repeated three times the same prayer: "Most Holy Trinity....." and then disappeared.

From that day onwards, Francisco and Jacinta felt a growing desire to receive Jesus present in the Eucharist and felt a compelling need to spend long periods of time before the tabernacle. "The hidden Jesus" was their favorite expression for the Blessed Sacrament.

On May 13, 1917, while the three children were pasturing their flock near the Cova da Iria, they witnessed an apparition of Our Lady, who ordered them to come back to that same place every thirteenth day of the month until October. In one of these apparitions, the Blessed Virgin showed them Hell.

Our Lady asked the children to pray and sacrifice for sinners, mostly by participating in the Mass and by reciting the Rosary.

15. Venerable Antonietta Meo (1930-1937)

This child, born in Rome to a very Catholic family, lived her short life afflicted with various illnesses.

Jesus in the Eucharist was the center of her life.

Antonietta prepared herself carefully for confession and waited for it anxiously: "Dear Jesus, I am very happy that tomorrow I'll go to confession...because the priest represents you at that moment, dear Jesus!"

The day before her First Communion, Antonietta wrote: "Dear Jesus, tell God the Father that I am very happy He inspired me to receive my First Communion on Christmas Day, because this is the day Jesus was born to save us and to die on the cross."

To those who told her how beautiful her white Communion dress was, she replied: "The dress is nice, but the important thing is for our soul's dress to be beautiful."

Jesus to her was Almighty God from whom she could ask many graces. On the day of her First Communion she listed the graces she wanted to ask for: "Dear Jesus in the Eucharist, I would like to receive three graces:

first, I want to become a saint, and this is the most important of my wishes; second, I would like you to give me souls to save; thirdly, I wish you would heal me and make me walk well; but this is not really very important."

After having received her First Communion on Christmas night, she wrote: "Dear Jesus in the Eucharist, I thank you because this year I received my First Communion and you came to stay in my heart."

After that night, Antonietta wanted to receive Communion every day and wrote to Jesus in a long letter: "Dear Jesus in the Eucharist, I love you so much.... Dear Jesus, I know you suffered much when you were a child! Every Sunday I want to go to Mass where the sacrifice of the cross is renewed and where you make a greater sacrifice, concealing yourself in the Sacrament of the Altar. Dear Jesus, I shall come to receive you every Sunday; I would like to receive you every day, but my mother won't take me to church."

When she couldn't go to church she made a spiritual communion and wrote to Jesus: "Dear Jesus, I cannot come to receive you in Holy Communion, but I would like you to come spiritually into my heart every morning."

As soon as she could, she offered Communions of reparation for sins, which Pope Pius XI had strongly recommended: "Dear Jesus, tomorrow I shall receive Holy Communion in reparation for the sins of men who don't want you."

Let us pray to this great little saint, asking her to help us to have the same devotion towards Jesus in the Eucharist.

16. Blessed Alexandrina Maria Da Costa (1904-1955)

Alexandrina Maria was born on March 30, 1904, in the city of Balasar, Portugal. At the young age of fourteen, Alexandrina threw herself from a window, four yards high, to escape the unwanted advances of three ill-intentioned men and to preserve her purity. As a consequence of this, Alexandrina was bedridden from the 14th of April 1925 on, and for the rest of her life remained there, never to move again.

One day, finding herself alone, Alexandrina was struck by a thought: "Christ, you are a prisoner within your tabernacles and I in my bed; we shall keep each other company." This marked the beginning of her mission to be the light of Christ.

In every Mass she offered herself to God together with Christ as a victim for the world's sinners. From Friday, October 3rd, 1938, until March 24th, 1942, she experienced the Passion of Our Lord 182 times. From 1942 until her death in 1955, she lived on the Eucharist alone, without any other food or drink. In 1943 her absolute refusal to eat was observed and verified by doctors from the Hospital Foce Del Duoro of Oporto.

After ten years of illness which she had offered up for the sins of the world and for the conversion of sinners, on the 30th of July, she had an apparition of Our Lord, who said to her: "I placed you in this world to live through the Eucharist and thus show the world its true worth: it is the light and salvation of the world. While you are here on earth, pray for the blind, the poor, and sinners. Guide them to my love; do not leave me alone in my tabernacles. I await souls that love me as you have loved me, but I have none! I have been forgotten and so I am hurt."

Mary, Mother of God, appeared to her on September 2nd, 1949, saying: "The world agonizes and dies in its own sins. I want prayers, I want penance! Wrap in my Rosary all those in the world whom you love!"

On September 13th, 1955, Alexandrina died, exclaiming: "I am happy because I am going to heaven. Sinners, sin no more; trample on my ashes, but do not offend Christ any longer." This is the essence of her life spent for the sins of the world.

The Eucharist increases charity and forms saints. Padre Pio used to say that if we understood the immense value of the Mass, the churches would be so full that we wouldn't be able to get in. Mother Teresa of Calcutta

understood that it is the Eucharist which helps us grow in charity. The Sisters of the Order she founded go to Mass and adore the Blessed Sacrament for an hour each day.